THE POWER OF UNEXPECTED MIRACLES

"A True Story About a Series of
Blessings in Disguise"

BETH ELKASSIH

These works are based on actual events. In certain cases, incidents,
characters, and timelines have been changed for dramatic purposes
to protect the privacy of the individuals.

DEDICATION

To My Mother

A strong and gentle soul who taught me to believe in God, believe
In hard work and always be kind and respectful to all.
I humbly aspire to be like her!

****

To Anyone Who Wants to Strengthen Their Faith

This book is dedicated to help you realize how 'amazing' you truly
are and your purpose in life. More importantly,
to believe or renew your belief in
God and Divine Intervention.

****

To All Mothers and Mothers-To-Be

I also dedicate this book to all Mothers from all cultures and
Religions in the world. Mothers all hold a common bond
not only being a miracle themselves, but caring
and nurturing 'little miracles'
throughout their lives.

****

To Anyone Suffering From Depression

For those of you are currently suffering from depression,
Especially Mothers dealing with post-partum depression, this
Book was written to you for inspiration and assurance
that 'this too will pass' and you will come
through to the other side
KNOWING you ARE both unique and special.
Unexpected miracles do occur everyday!

ACKNOWLEDGEMENTS

I first give thanks to God for giving me the courage and the strength to 'go the distance' in sharing my story to others. I firmly believe I was guided by Him throughout this incredible journey.

****

I want to give the greatest of gratitude for the love and support of my immediate family – my husband Abed, and daughters, Renae Patricia, Layla Saphia and Nadean Elizabeth.

****

I am also thankful for other family members who were a major part of this journey. Thank you Aunt Nadean, Cousin Betsy, Aunt Carol, Aunt Sue, my Sisters, Andrea, Theresa, Ava and Stasia, and my Brothers, Tony, Jeff and Ben. A special 'shout out' to my Sister Ava, for her loyal support and encouragement during this traumatic time of my life.

****

I have been blessed with so many friends, both whom I've known all my life and those who I've met recently. Thank you to Mernell King, Elaine Platz, Gayle Wilt, Michelle Sillery, Luz Seranno-Reyes, Poovanesh Pather, Ellen Ravkind, Mona and Trevor Somer Lane, Jane Cook, Mary Johnson, Carolyn Howard and Nichole Peters. Also thanks to those who have directly or indirectly assisted me in completing this labor of love.

****

I am really fortunate to have Muhammad Umair Qureshi, creator of *www.zulzan.com*, cross my life path and journey beginning in October 2018. He has not only been the best *web developer* I've ever worked with, but his inspiration and humble guidance to encourage me to write this much needed book does not go unnoticed. I will be eternally grateful for his loyalty and support. He is not only my business associate but a true friend. Thank you Umair.

For more information:

www.zulzan.com

www.wpstairs.com

TABLE OF CONTENTS

INTRODUCTION

The word *'miracle'* is often used to characterize any beneficial event that is statistically unlikely but not contrary to the laws of nature. Often when we think of miracles, we think of those who have survived a natural disaster, or simply a 'wonderful' occurrence, regardless of likelihood, such as the birth of a newborn child.

Other such miracles might include the survival of a previously diagnosed terminal illness or escaping a life-threatening situation or 'beating the odds'. Some people might label this as just a coincidence. Many others would emphatically believe these events exclusively happen by Divine Intervention.

Coincidence, Synchronicity or Divine Intervention

Divine intervention is all around us and we need to learn to recognize it and be open to unexpected events and see the *'big picture'*. **"The Power of Unexpected Miracles"** is a true story based upon synchronistic events, including the unlikeliness of *'the rudeness of a stranger'*. This story is both powerful and thought-provoking.

You will be awed and moved by what 'every day events' we take for granted really mean. By the end of this story, you will learn to be grateful for all that happens in your everyday life. You will learn how important it is to be forgiving and not judgmental in the understanding and acceptance of unexplainable events on a daily basis.

Fair warning. This story will inspire you emotionally. You will be totally immersed in the realization of the power of unexpected miracles... ***Divine Intervention!*** It is truly life-changing.

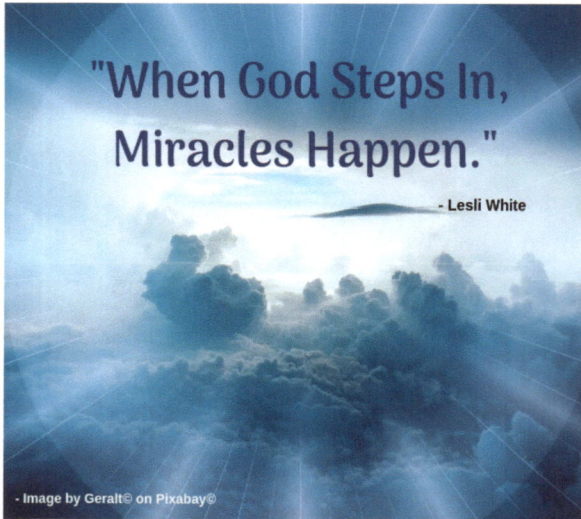

"When God Steps In, Miracles Happen."

- Lesli White

- Image by Geralt© on Pixabay©

CHAPTER ONE – ARRIVAL OF A MIRACLE

I remember it well. It was a Tuesday early afternoon, January 20, 1998, to be precise. My husband and I were en route to our local hospital here in Arlington, Texas. Today was the day for the pre-scheduled delivery of our third child, a daughter. She was to be named "Nadean Elizabeth" after my mother's oldest sister.

Since I had had two previous C-sections with my two other daughters, Renae Patricia (Patty) and Layla Saphia, this would also be a routine C-section. Or so I thought! While being prepared for surgery in the maternity ward, I anxiously recalled the visit with my doctor the day before.

I was considered an 'old mother' (in two weeks I was turning 41) and had a previous history of high blood pressure. I was used to the every-other-week sonogram performed. Yesterday had been a bit different, however. The sonographer took a little bit more time than usual. I have to say, in reflection, I thought something might be of concern. When I asked her if everything was okay, she assured me, 'Oh yes, your baby is fully developed and very healthy.' Nevertheless, she instructed me to get dressed and my doctor would see me in his office.

I was exactly 37 weeks along and my doctor was pleased with the development of my daughter. That said, there was no real reason to wait so he was going to go ahead and schedule the C-section as soon as an opening was available at the nearest hospital. He mentioned something about 'being out of town' and that he wanted to be sure to be on-hand for the actual surgery. I didn't think anything of it and was promptly scheduled for the next day.

Waiting for Surgery

So... back to the maternity prep room. The anesthesiologist came by and wanted to discuss the type of anesthesia my doctor had instructed him to give. He explained that instead of an epidural, he would be giving me a 'spinal block'. I inquired as to why, since I had had an epidural with my two other daughters and it worked fabulously. Why change now?

He assured me that this was a better option in light of my ongoing health issues with high blood pressure. Also, he mentioned something about my being uber sensitive to the epidural medicine... I didn't quite understand, but hey, he was a professional in his field and what right did I have to question him? So... I endured the somewhat painful procedure of having a spinal block administered.

I had asked my younger sister, Ava, to be present and she was happy to do so. Unfortunately, my mother would not be with me. She had been present at the birth of my other two daughters, but she had passed six months ago, due to the insidious disease known as pancreatic cancer. Needless to say, I missed her dearly, but it was comforting to know my sister Ava would be with me.

Unfortunately, Ava got tied up in traffic that late afternoon and was delayed. My wonderful mother-in-law was present and I did appreciate her being there. She was still praying that I would have a son, even though approximately 10 sonograms and an amniocentesis procedure had confirmed I would be giving her a grand-daughter! But pray she did!

When 5:30 p.m. arrived, it was time for the surgery. My sister had not shown up but my husband got a message from her saying she was on her way. Not to worry, my attending nurse assured me that once my sister arrived, she would immediately escort her into the surgical room to be with me and my husband.

So, there I was lying flat on the hospital surgical table waiting what seemed like forever for the anesthesiologist, my doctor and an assistant doctor to proceed. I was asked if I wanted to go under or stay awake. Of course, I wanted to stay awake to see the birth of my daughter! What kind of question was that?!?

I heard the anesthesiologist make an off-the-cuff remark saying that I had the 'quickest surgeon in town'. Apparently, he performed C-sections in record time! My husband asked him what his average time was and he proudly (and smugly I might add...) stated "no more than 20 minutes tops!'

The Delivery

The surgery began. My husband was standing at my right side, next to my head. My sister hadn't arrived but the surgery had to begin. Okay, deep breath, here we go…

I had been through this same type of surgery two times before, but it was obvious from the onset, this surgery was not going to be routine. I was awake and alert, but the screen across my sternum blocked my view. After the first five minutes, I noted that no one was saying anything. It was completely silent! I immediately piped up and asked, 'Is everything okay?' I was told yes, that my daughter would be in my arms in no time.

The look on my husband's face said otherwise. Suddenly, there was rapid knocking at the door. Next thing I remember was the nurse hurrying to the door and leaving. I knew it had to be my sister who had arrived late. But for whatever reason, they wouldn't let her in. (Later I found out, she was furious and upset, as she had been told she would be brought in immediately.)

Nadean Elizabeth Arrives

Oh, what joy it was to hear the first sounds of my dear Nadean Elizabeth as she was briefly and hurriedly presented to me! I barely got to hold her but I did manage a kiss before the nurse swept her away from me. She said they needed to take her to 'bathe and check her out'. That had never happened before! I always had the luxury of holding my other two daughters during the post-surgical closures. And my husband had the privilege of 'cutting the umbilical cord' for Patty and Layla, but he didn't do it this time.

This isn't my first rodeo so now I was getting a little concerned. The time on the clock showed 45 minutes had passed. Wasn't that a good 25 minutes over and above the doctor's average?

Suddenly, I began to feel extremely nauseous. The anesthesiologist told me that the spinal block was wearing off and it would be necessary to 'put me under' to complete the surgery. My husband looked confused but he told me not to worry and everything would be okay. So… I went under…

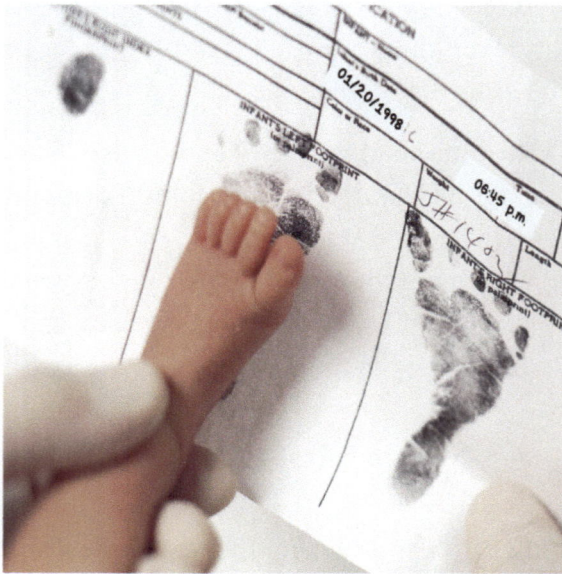

Waking Up in Post-Partum Recovery

I awoke in a state of confusion and discomfort. Once again, things were not the same as they were when I delivered my other two daughters. I was placed in a semi-private regular hospital room after the surgery. This time, I was in the 'Surgical Observation Room,' and I didn't understand why.

Ava was beside herself still wiping the tears from being denied to join me in the surgical room. My husband was exhausted, as this was Ramadan for him and he had been fasting all day. It was about 7:30 p.m. I asked to see my baby but I was told she was resting comfortably in the hospital nursery and there would be plenty of time to be with her.

My husband explained that there had been some complications with my delivery. I was amazed when he told me that when they opened me up, the entire placenta was lying on top of my uterus! Nadean Elizabeth was delivered within six minutes and she was fine. But for me, they had to take more time to complete the surgery and decided it was best to put me under.

My doctor arrived and reiterated what my husband had said. He further explained that my placenta had grown outside my uterus, but my baby remained safely intact inside and was a healthy 5 lb. 15 oz. beautiful girl. He also made it a point to advise me that it would be best not to try and have any more children. (I found this a curious statement because believe me, at age 41, this definitely would be my last.) In any event, he said he needed me to be in 24-hour observation to make sure everything was okay. Then he left.

It was comforting to see my sister but she couldn't stay long and had to leave and get back to her own family. I understood. My husband left briefly to find something to nibble on in the hospital cafeteria, and I was left alone...

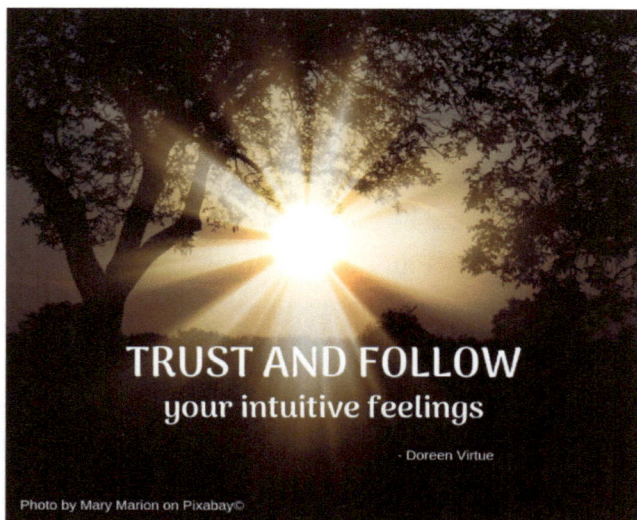

TRUST AND FOLLOW
your intuitive feelings

· Doreen Virtue

Photo by Mary Marion on Pixabay©

Something's Not Right!

I was hooked up to a monitoring machine which was measuring my blood pressure and pulse. I couldn't explain why, but I started having this ***intuitive feeling*** that things were not quite right. It was evident that the spinal block and anesthesia had worn off.

I could feel everything. Now for those of you who are not mothers, let me explain that in recovery after giving childbirth, your body goes into what is known as *post-partum contractions*. And just like regular contractions, there is a threshold where the pain reduces until the next contraction arrives.

But in my case, the pain did NOT go away. It just continued to escalate in intensity. My husband had not yet come back. I looked up at the monitor. The blood pressure numbers were headed in the wrong direction. They were going down. Likewise, I noted that my heart rate was going up in the other direction. Now I'm not a doctor, but let me tell you, I instinctively *knew* that there was something going on... and it wasn't good.

Finally, my husband returned. He complained that there was nothing worthwhile to eat and he was going to leave and stop by his mother's since they usually have a 'feast' when breaking the fast for Ramadan. Oh no. He was not going to leave if I had anything to do with it!

So... I pleaded with him. "Abed, I don't feel right and the pain is not getting any better. Will you please go and get a nurse to check on me?" You know what he said to me?!? I couldn't believe my ears. He tiredly said, "Beth, you've been through this two other times. You just need to toughen it up!"

Wrong thing to say, my dear husband!!! "Look, the pain is intolerable. My blood pressure is dropping and my heart rate is rising." He just stood there in silence. I couldn't wait one more second. I needed help and I needed help NOW. It was at this point, I took hold of his wrist and literally dug my fingernails in making sure to make a lasting imprint.

"There is something majorly wrong. And I need you to go get somebody and I need you to get somebody NOW!" I shouted at him in a not so quiet voice!

Abed left and the next thing I knew a nurse came in, checked my heart rate and shouted 'STAT'. Within 60 seconds, there were 3-4 more medical personnel in my room. When the anesthesiologist arrived, I told him that the pain was so intense that all I wanted was to be knocked out. He instructed the nurses to get an IV started asap! My veins were 'flat' and unresponsive, and they couldn't insert an IV needle. The doctor arrived and shouted, "Why doesn't she have an IV?" When they told him why, he was obviously upset. "Then she needs a central line!"

While the doctor was checking my heart rate through his stethoscope, I pleaded with him. "What is going on?!" He told me I must try my best to calm down and relax. He explained I needed immediate surgery, but that things would be okay. It wasn't too assuring, let me tell you!

I told the doctor the pain was too much – to please just knock me out. He explained they must first complete the Central Line and then I would be made comfortable. In that instant, my body heaved. Nausea came over me and what felt like hot liquid gushed from deep inside me down my legs. I was hemorrhaging. I gave one last look at my doctor and grabbed his arm and said:

"DO NOT LET ANYTHING BAD HAPPEN TO ME!"

At that point, I saw a nurse tell my husband he needed to leave. With every bit of energy I could muster, I gave him a parting look and told him *"Be sure to take care of my daughters."* They had to literally push my husband out of the room.

Finally, the central line was successfully placed and I felt myself enter a deep and relaxing state of mind… the pain was over. I could feel nothing and lost consciousness.

"I'm ever so thankful to my husband, sister, family and friends for all your support in my time of need."
- Beth Elkassih

Image by Canva©

Waking Up in the ICU Room

My eyes were fluttering. I was struggling to open my eyes but they felt as if someone had placed a ton of bricks on top of them. I felt something inside my mouth and when I finally was fully awake, I saw two plastic tubes up my nose. I couldn't speak! I saw my husband and my sister Ava. Her eyes were red and swollen. I groggily tried to muster a sound but nothing came out of my voice box. I reached out and touched my husband's arm and startled him. He immediately took my hand and softly told me to just rest and that everything was going to be okay.

My sister saw my anxiety and confusion and gave me a small notepad and a pencil. I haphazardly scribbled, "What happened?" Ava told me that they had to do an emergency life-saving hysterectomy. She explained that they had to give massive blood transfusions as I had lost 8-10 pints of blood. (the human body has an average of 9-12 units in total volume.) She gave me a long and tight bear hug and tells me not to worry about anything.

A nurse arrived to check my vital signs. She immediately removed my breathing tube and she showed me how to use the morphine drip to control my pain. The nurse stated how happy she was to see me awake and fully responsive. I appreciated what she said but all I wanted was to see my baby daughter. The nurse explained that because I'm in the ICU, I would not be able to have the baby with me. But she would alert the attending physician and hopefully, I would be transferred to a regular private hospital room soon.

Although I had been 'out' for over 8 hours or more, I still found myself both physically and mentally exhausted. But no time to rest. Only 15 minutes or so had passed when everybody started showing up! Don't get me wrong, I love all my family and in-laws but all I wanted to do was rest and see my baby. Why couldn't they understand that?

My mother-in-law arrived with her daughters, Nada and Ghada. My brother-in-law Mahmoud arrived with his wife May. I only had my sister Ava from my side of the family and I begged her to stay. Why was everybody looking at me like 'a deer in headlights!' I was totally taken aback when Abed's brother, Mahmoud, came over and whispered, "Don't have another baby. Don't try for a son. It's not worth it. You've been through enough!" Why are we having this conversation, I asked myself.

Later, I found out I had been in surgery for over six hours and according to my husband, they had me upside down to keep the blood in my brain. Long story short, I finally realized that by the grace of God, I was truly lucky to be alive. And my beautiful, vibrant daughter had arrived in this world healthy and without a scratch on her.

I was transferred into my own private hospital room and everyone finally dispersed. I was alone again. But this time, I finally was given my daughter to hold and caress. Despite the ongoing pain of not one, but two major surgeries, I was in total bliss and joy! I was a mother again for the third time.

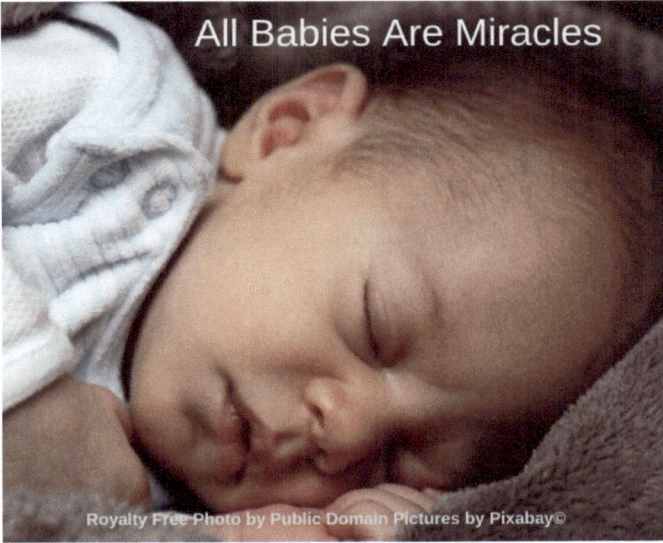

All Babies Are Miracles

Royalty Free Photo by Public Domain Pictures by Pixabay©

CHAPTER TWO – 16 MONTHS EARLIER

Life was somewhat chaotic and stressful when I was discharged two weeks after the arrival of beautiful Nadean. You would think that being in the comfort of my home, it would have allowed me to fully relax. Unfortunately, this was not the case.

I had a one and one-half-year-old toddler (Layla) who was enjoying her newly acquired skill of walking everywhere! And I don't know what I would have done if I hadn't had my oldest daughter, Patty! She helped out as much as an 8-year-old could. I loved my three daughters and truly felt blessed.

But soon, despite my efforts to be the best wife and mother of three, I found myself in a place of despair. I wasn't sleeping well and sleep deprivation took a tremendous toll on my psyche. Coupled with trying to recover from two major surgeries, missing my recently passed mother, and just dealing with life in general, I fell into a depression. It saddens me to say, that dark hole opened up and swallowed me whole. I could not cope.

Those of you who are mothers and have been down this road, know exactly how it feels. This was not the everyday baby 'blues.' This was chronic post-partum depression.

As a result, recovery from the hysterectomy and C-section would take about a good four months or so. The post-partum depression, on the other hand, took another 2-3 months to recover from. But it's all good. This allowed me to take the necessary time to reflect on all the events that took place. Many a time, I would find myself staring down at my daughter Nadean and each time I did, I recalled one moment after the other that contributed to the little miracle I was holding.

Jedo

We never know what life has in store for us. Sometimes, life has a way of smacking you in the face. Sixteen months before Nadean was born, my father-in-law passed away. He was very special to me. He had lived with my husband and I off and on for the previous three and a half years. It was so great to have him live with us during his final years. Seven years earlier, he had also spent some time with Abed and me in Ballwin, Missouri, after Patty came along in the summer of 1990.

He was Patty's caregiver while I worked as a Corporate Software Trainer. He was a lifesaver. Many times I found myself having to go out of town for at least a week at a time. He doted on her and really was a great influence on her life in her toddler years. Many days I would come home from the airport and I would see Patty sitting in the sink (yes, the kitchen sink.) She would be giggling as 'Jedo' (aka grandpa) was preparing the family meal.

My husband and I were blessed a second time when my father-in-law came to live with us again, this time in Arlington, Texas. He continued delighting my daughter Patty and was present when our second daughter came along, Miss Layla. In fact, we named Layla with the middle name of Saphia (yes everyone, it's spelled correctly) in respect of my father-in-law's mother. Layla was indeed a handful, but my father-in-law never minded. He loved playing with her and as it turned out, both Patty and Layla brought him much needed joy during what turned out to be the last five months of his life.

My father-in-law passed away in September 1996. He died of a massive heart attack as a result of his diabetes and congestive heart failure. I don't have to tell you this broke my heart. I was so fond of my father-in-law and I felt I took him too much for granted. The grieving process was a struggle for both my husband and myself to get through.

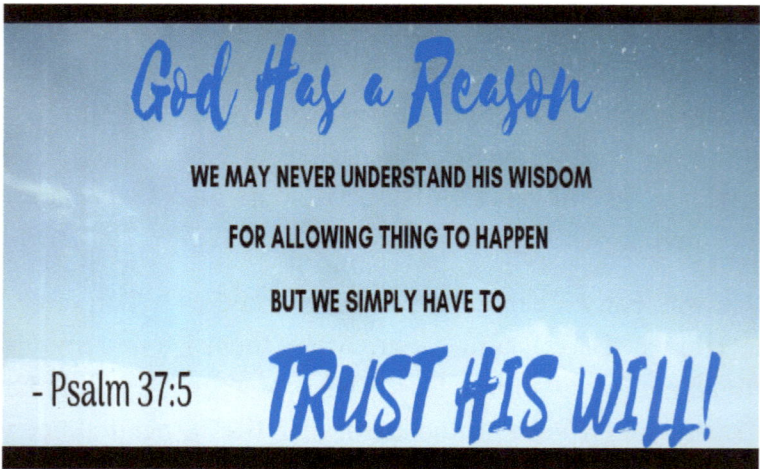

God Has a Reason

WE MAY NEVER UNDERSTAND HIS WISDOM

FOR ALLOWING THING TO HAPPEN

BUT WE SIMPLY HAVE TO

TRUST HIS WILL!

- Psalm 37:5

The Dreaded Phone Call

Then just a short two months later, I got the worst phone call of my life. It was my mother. She was scheduled for what originally was a routine gall bladder surgery. I had asked earlier in the week if she wanted me to come to Missouri to be with her during her recovery, but she said she would be fine with the help of my father.

You know that gnawing feeling you get when you just *know* there's a note of doom in the air? My mother didn't even have to say a word, I knew this conversation was not going to be good. Sure enough, her tone was somber and I could hear the fear in her voice.

"I'm so sorry, Honey, but I have some bad news to share with you" she began.

In preparation for her upcoming gall bladder surgery, my Mother was admitted the day before for some routine procedures. They did bloodwork and scheduled a sonogram. Now instead of prepping for gall bladder surgery, a new surgical team would be doing the removal of a tumor inside her pancreas. There was no speculation, my Mom was not suffering from a gall bladder attack. She was suffering from pancreatic cancer.

Three stressful hours later I found myself with my sister Ava on a non-stop flight to St. Louis. Nothing was going to stop us from being with our mother in her time of need.

On November 2, 1996, my mother was officially diagnosed with Stage 3 pancreatic cancer. The oncology surgeon was optimistic and said he felt they were able to get all the cancerous tumor out. Now it was a matter of having chemo and radiation treatments. He advised that with these treatments, my mom had a good outlook of possibly five good years left.

Since I wasn't working, I immediately volunteered to stay on in Missouri to help my mother out and take care of my father around the house as well. My husband drove up from Texas and brought little Layla with him. It was one thing to leave Patty at home with my husband, but it was another with a six and a half-month-old. Layla needed my constant attention and my mother was the one who insisted that she come. As it turns out, my exuberant Layla was a pure delight with her constant giggles and unconditional love only a child can give to their grandma. It was definitely a good decision.

So for the next ten weeks, I stayed at home helping out while my mother went through all her chemo and radiation treatments. She got through them and it was refreshing to hear the oncology doctor giving her permission to travel. She wanted to have a long trip visiting her three sons in California. Although she had dropped quite a bit of weight, it was nice seeing her smile again. And two weeks before I returned back to Texas, Layla was crawling her way into everything she could find at home. Drove her grandfather nuts!

The Anvil Drops

After mother completed all the scheduled chemo and radiation treatments. She wanted to spend some quality time in California recuperating and visiting with her three sons, Tony, Jeff and Ben. And like the trouper she was, she didn't waste any time planning her trip. In mid-January 1997, she and my Dad drove from Missouri to San Diego, California.

My younger brother, Jeff, and his wife, who happens to be an oncology nurse, kept in touch with me on a regular basis regarding how Mom was holding up. He frequently expressed concern over her obvious increasing fatigue and she was losing weight -- weight she couldn't afford to lose. He was worried about her. After two weeks, the dreadful phone call came to haunt me a second time...

This time when my brother called, it was to let me know that Mom had been admitted to Scripts Hospital in La Jolla, California. And more than likely, she wouldn't be leaving any time soon. Turns out my mom's cancer had returned with a vengeance.

My heart sank as soon as I heard the words that her cancer had metastasized. This couldn't be happening. Didn't the oncology doctor in Missouri tell me and my brothers and sisters that she would have five good years left?!? What's going on? This isn't fair. It had to be a mistake. But it wasn't. It felt as if a one-ton anvil had dropped on my shoulders. I was devastated.

"We spend so much time asking God to cure us of our hardships. But we never stop to consider that our hardships are curing us."

- Yasmin Mogahed

Photo by _____ ©   Designed in Canva ©

Hospice Care in Missouri

Despite it all, my mother remained strong and devout in her unshakable belief in God, she accepted her prognosis bravely. However, she wasn't about to live her last days stuck in an oncology ward in a hospital. Nope, she was going to go back to Missouri and be in her home, where she belonged. And believe me, once my mom made up her mind, nothing was going to stand in her way.

My sister Ava and I made immediate arrangements to take turns to go to Missouri and help out with the daily care of my mother. Our older sister, Andrea, just lived an hour away, but was limited in the time she could be there as she couldn't get time off from her work. Since I wasn't working at the time, I didn't mind at all to stay as much as I needed to.

Thus began, the arduous task of hospice care. There was much to learn about taking proper care. My Mom did not want to be hooked up to any IVs etc. so she was given morphine drops which were administered orally to ease her pain. Her appetite decreased but she managed to always want her favorite dessert, tapioca.

After about a week, my youngest sister, Stasia, came to help out from Phoenix, Arizona. It was good to see her and she was a breath of fresh air to be around. Since my mother really did require 24/7 care, we took turns being next to her bedside.

One important note. I would be totally amiss if I didn't mention my wonderful Aunt Nadean and cousin Betsy. They also played a major role in taking time to come on a daily basis to be with us all. My mom was conscious and alert for the most part and she spent her last days actually reminiscing about the great times she had during her lifetime. And believe me, she didn't hesitate to give each one of us children, her advice on how we needed to live our lives…

"Love is stronger than death even though it can't stop death from happening, but no matter how hard death tries, it can't separate people from LOVE."

- Photo by Fnora©
by Pixabay©

- Unknown Author

CHAPTER THREE – WHAT DID YOU SAY MOM SAID?!

I'll never forget the morning when my younger sister Stasia ran into the kitchen where I was preparing breakfast. "You won't believe what Mom just said to me!" She continued, "She says you're going to have another baby!"

My dear sister. She obviously misunderstood. My mother was under the influence of morphine and there was no telling what she would say. "Oh Stasia, don't you know Mom was probably telling YOU that you were going to have another baby."

"I don't think so. I heard what I heard", she insisted.

I wouldn't give in. "Look Stasia, I'm 40 years old. It took me almost six years to even get pregnant with Layla. There's no way I'm going to have another child. Mom wasn't talking about me. She was talking about YOU. Why do I know that? Because you're 10 years younger than me and you only have Marrissa and she's the one who needs another baby brother or sister, not me!"

"Whatever Beth, but I know what I heard".

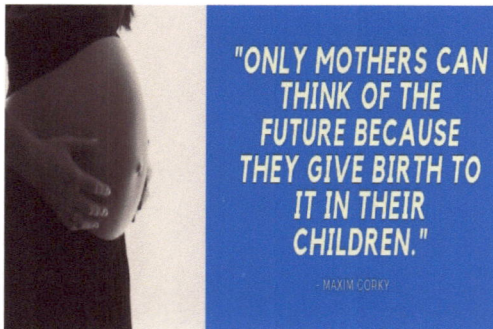

"ONLY MOTHERS CAN THINK OF THE FUTURE BECAUSE THEY GIVE BIRTH TO IT IN THEIR CHILDREN."

- MAXIM GORKY

CHAPTER FOUR – JUNE 2, 1997

Exactly six months, two days from the date my mother was diagnosed with pancreatic cancer, she passed away. I was present with her passing, along with my older sister Andrea, brother Tony, baby sister Stasia, my father, Aunt Nadean and the county nurse. The suffering had stopped and my mother was on her way to Heaven to be with the angels and Almighty God.

The presence of my Mom's spirit could be felt radiating throughout the living room where she laid. It was an indescribable feeling. It was as if God was ever so present and exuding so much love in the air! This feeling or whatever you want to call it, was and is unforgettable. God does exist and there is no question there is a Heaven and an afterlife.

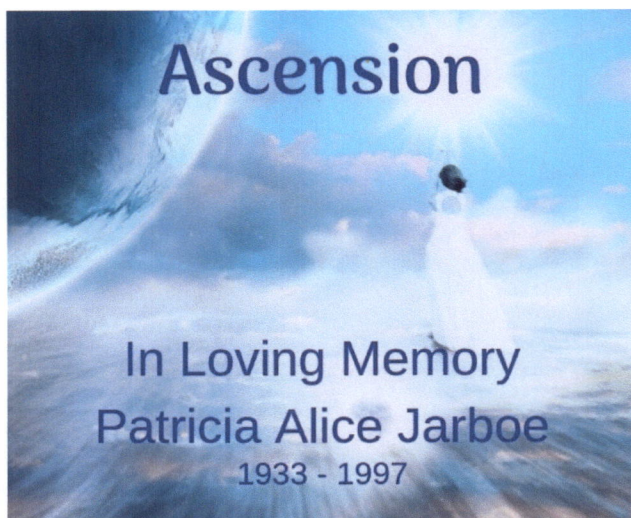

Ascension

In Loving Memory
Patricia Alice Jarboe
1933 - 1997

CHAPTER FIVE – LIFE GOES ON

Returning to Texas and being back with my entire family was very much needed. It had been a long six months of being emotionally and physically 'spent' with everything that had taken place. By this time, Layla was walking. This little girl didn't stop walking from the time she woke up to the time she went to bed. But I didn't mind.

I also got to spend quality time again with my darling Patty. She was so understanding and patient through this challenging time. Despite being just eight years old, she already had experienced the death of both her beloved grandfather and now her grandmother. She was so mature and loving. She made me proud.

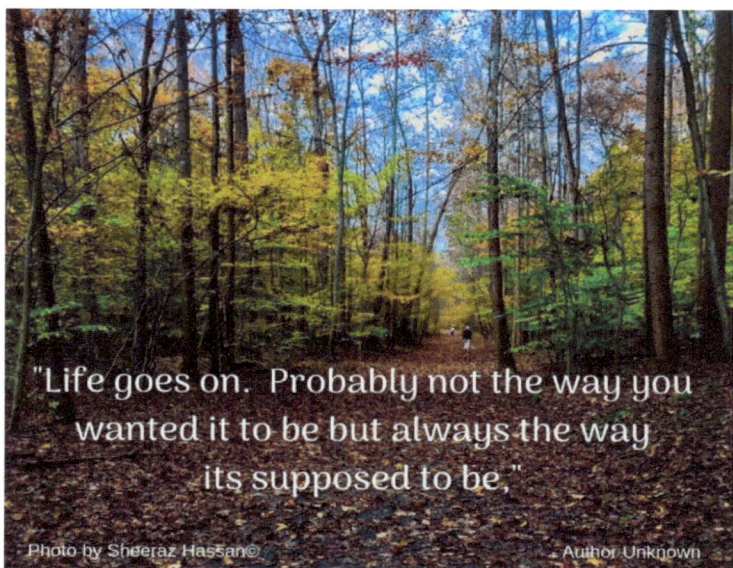

"Life goes on. Probably not the way you wanted it to be but always the way its supposed to be."

Photo by Sheeraz Hassan©   - Author Unknown

What's Going On With My Body!

About two weeks after returning home, it appeared that I had started my period. It was somewhat early but with everything I went through and still being in the grieving process, I didn't think anything of it. That said, I noted my period only lasted 3 days, which was pretty much normal.

Seven days later, I noticed I had some 'spots' and flowed a little for another 2 days and then it stopped. Again, I chalked it up to the grieving process just messing up my cycle.

However, when the third time of having these issues occurred, I got a little concerned. I immediately picked up the phone and called my sister, Ava, who lived in Keller Texas, about 30 minutes from me. When I told her what was going on, she immediately scolded me and said, "Beth! You need to get this checked out! We just lost our mom to cancer. I don't want anything bad to happen to you! This isn't right."

"Okay, okay", I told her. "But it's a known fact that in times of stress, our periods can get out of whack, right?"

"Beth! I'm not a doctor and neither are you! Promise me, you'll make a doctor's appointment, like tomorrow….. please…"

A Serendipity Blessing!

The next day I managed to have an appointment scheduled in between an already booked schedule for my doctor. But I insisted on being seen and wouldn't mind waiting just to get in. When I finally got to see my doctor, it was a pretty brief examination. He agreed that probably the grieving process combined with stress contributed to my condition but it was important to find out what was going on. He ordered some bloodwork.

I was feeling rather fatigued for the remainder of the day and slept most of the next day as well. It was a Friday afternoon and around 5:30 p.m., the phone rang. To my surprise, it was actually my doctor on the line. He advised me that the bloodwork came back in. He said he had some good news and not so good news…

"Mrs. Elkassih, the lab report came back and believe it or not but you are pregnant!" (What! He had to be mistaken.)

"But, the not so good news is that I suspect you may be in the beginning stages of miscarrying." (No!!! This can't be so!)

He continued, "It's important that you rest as much as possible but if you begin to bleed again or start having abdominal pain, to go to the emergency room right away. Regardless, I need for you to come in first thing Monday morning so I can perform a sonogram."

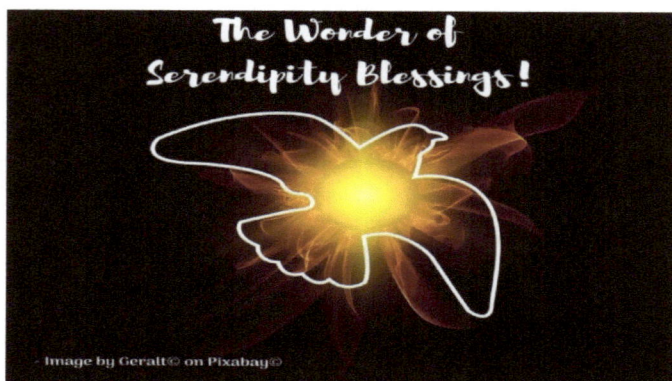

The Wonder of Serendipity Blessings!

Image by Geralt© on Pixabay©

Monday's Sonogram

Of course, I had to call Ava immediately after I hung up the phone with the doctor.

"Ava! You won't believe this! " I quickly told her.

"What are you talking about Beth?" she exclaimed.

"I just got off the phone with my doctor and he tells me I'm pregnant!", I excitedly shouted at her!

After discussing everything at length with my sister, I made the decision it was best not to say anything to my husband at this time. I didn't want to get his hopes up, knowing that I might end up miscarrying.

Instead, when he came home after on Friday, I told him that the bloodwork came back indicating I was anemic (which I was by the way). Furthermore, I was advised to rest as much as possible over the weekend and to come back Monday morning for a follow-up visit. He didn't question anything.

Monday morning arrived and I carefully drove myself to the doctor's office. My doctor performed the sonogram. Initially, he didn't say anything. He just took his time doing a thorough examination. Finally, he broke the silence and said:

"Congratulations Mrs. Elkassih. Not only are you pregnant but you are three months along! Would you like to have a photo of the sonogram so you can share with your husband?"

I was flabbergasted! I never expected to get pregnant again. Let alone finding out I was three months along! You see, it took almost six years to get pregnant with my second daughter, Layla. Why would I ever think I could get pregnant a third time, let alone just 10 months after Layla was born! And when did this wonderful conception take place anyway?

I counted backward. Yes! I remembered. My husband came up to Missouri one weekend and brought Patty with him to surprise me. That had to be *THE* time this miracle took place!

I was elated but then reality came back to me. My doctor said that since I was 40 at the time and with my prior history of high blood pressure, I was 'high risk'. Although typically miscarriages occur within the three month time period of early pregnancy, it could still occur. He cautioned me not to get too excited just yet.

He advised I would need to be totally off my feet and rest as much as possible. I would also need to be monitored every other week. If I could get past the 4-5 month period, then I would probably be out of the woods of having a potential miscarriage.

At this point, it didn't matter what my doctor said. *I knew with all my being, I was going to have this baby! Why did I think this? Because my Mother said I was going to have another baby, remember?!*

So, with the sonogram photo in hand, I decided to pay an unexpected trip to see my husband at work and take him out to lunch. I'll never forget his face when I arrived.

"What are you doing here?", he asked.

"I can't surprise my husband once in a while and take you out to lunch?", I responded.

"Okay, what's the problem. There must be something wrong." (What's up with husbands thinking their wives have an ulterior motive when we're just trying to be nice!)

"Yes, I do have something to tell you. But let's have lunch first." After we ordered, I couldn't wait any longer. "I have something to show you, honey".

I took out the sonogram photo and handed it to him. He just stared at it. Not a word… just complete silence for about a whole minute. Then he finally looks up and quietly whispers, "Is this what I think it is?"

My husband may whisper, but this isn't my M.O. I exuberantly exclaimed in the most euphoric voice I had, "Abed! Yes, we're going to have another baby!"

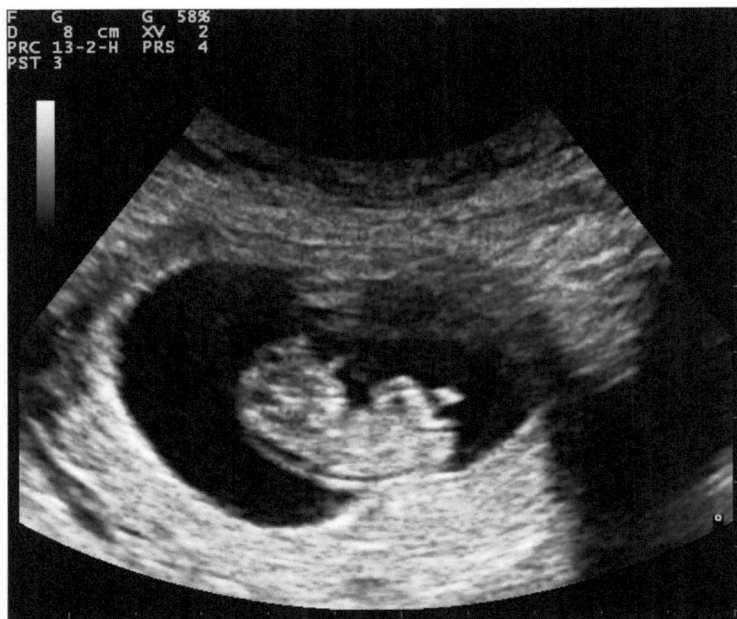

Divine Intervention or Just Premonition?

I could hardly contain myself while driving back home after having that great celebration lunch with my husband. I needed to call my sister Stasia in Arizona to let her know she was right all along. I could hardly wait to get her on the phone!

Chills continued to run up my spine. The full realization that my Mother *knew* prior to her passing, someway, somehow. This was totally absolute proof to me that God is very much real and the angels and/or God had to have had a hand in making this so!

"Stasia! You were so right. You won't believe what I have to tell you!" I just found out I'm pregnant! And not only am I pregnant but I'm three months along! "

She gasped. "Well, I told you that that's what Mom said. You wouldn't believe me!" my sister reminded me. At that moment, I burst into tears. My sister broke down as well as we both 'felt the presence' of our Mother right there with us over the telephone. It was magical. It was transforming. This exact same feeling was the same one we both experienced at the precise moment our Mother died. She was obviously present with us. And oh how I missed her!

Divine Intervention or Just Premonition?

- Sunrays by Maraco Roosink© on Pixabay

CHAPTER SIX – THE RUDENESS OF A STRANGER

For the next couple of months, I did as my doctor instructed me to do. I rested as much as possible and tried to eat healthily as well. For some reason, I craved eggs with this pregnancy as I had with my previous two.

I had routine office visits every other week. In the fifth month, I had an amniocentesis. This is when my husband and I were informed that we would be having a third daughter! I already had her name picked out. It would be in honor of my Aunt Nadean Elizabeth Wood, who was with my mother and me every day during her chemo and radiation treatments and during the heart-breaking weeks leading up to her passing.

I'm not going to sugar coat it. I struggled with this pregnancy all throughout carrying my future daughter. Unlike a lot of younger mothers who truly enjoy their pregnancies, mine was somewhat difficult. Nevertheless, I wouldn't trade it for anything in the world.

One late afternoon, about 31 weeks along, I started experiencing what I originally thought were phantom 'Braxton Hicks' contractions. However, I soon realized that this abdominal pain wasn't getting any better, but significantly worse.

Late Night Trip to the ER

With the urging of my husband, I called the 'doctor on call' and was advised to go straight to the emergency room to find out what was going on. When I arrived, I was given a shot of Demerol to ease

THE POWER OF UNEXPECTED MIRACLES

the pain. Also, I went through the usual lab workup and even endured another sonogram. After it became apparent that the pain was
not getting any better, the attending ER doctor advised me that he
was keeping me overnight as my Primary Care Physician wanted to
personally check me out in the morning.

I Don't Know What All The Fuss Is...

I was placed in what they called an 'observation' room. When
the nurse came in to check on me, she explained that per the doctor's
orders, she was instructed I would need an IV. I hate IVs.

I told the nurse I didn't want it. But she further advised that
evidently, my doctor might need to 'go in' and take a look to see
what was going on inside and that this was part of the prep work. I
still didn't want one. But she just ignored me and left to get that
dreaded 'needle'...

Several white curtains surrounded the area around my hospital
bed and the immediate area I was placed in. And as such, you could
hear everything pass the curtain divider. As it turns out, I could hear
my nurse speaking to another nurse as clear as day.

I couldn't believe my ears when I overheard her say, "I don't
know what all the fuss is. She's just am 'old' mother and probably
is just passing gas!"

Taking Matters Into My Own Hands

Well... how *'rude'* was that?!? She didn't even know me and
certainly, this was so inappropriate, let alone unprofessional. Then

33

I realized that the 'pain' had somewhat subsided. I made the decision to leave. Yes, to leave.

I told my husband I was feeling a lot better and simply wanted to go home. Of course, I had to sign a 'waiver' to be released, but I did and am I ever so thankful for making that decision. I promised the ER doctor that I would just rest on my couch and make an appointment with my own physician for the next day.

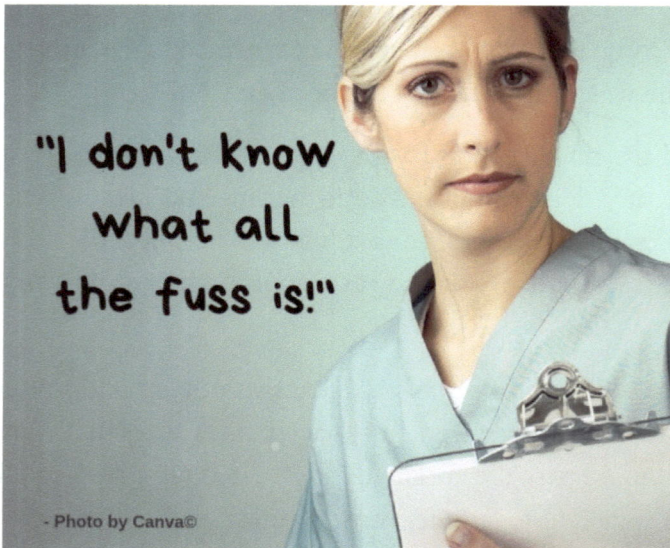

"I don't know what all the fuss is!"

- Photo by Canva©

Miracle Day – January 20, 1998

Fast forward five more weeks, January 20, 1998. It was a cold Tuesday morning. I was scheduled for another C-section, as my two previous babies had been 'breech' and required C-sections. As mentioned in chapter one, when my doctor opened me up, my entire 'placenta' was lying on top of my uterus! (This is known as 'placenta percreta' for those of you in the medical field.) Evidently, the 'placenta' had torn a hole through my uterine wall. Fortunately, my daughter Nadean was delivered quickly and suffered no health complications. In fact today, she is a vibrant, beautiful 21-year-old!

In chapter one, I detailed what took place that fateful night. After going through a life-saving hysterectomy, I ended up staying in the hospital for two long weeks. While I was in recovery, one of the attending physicians checked in on me to see how I was doing. You won't believe what she told me!

Thank God for that Rude Nurse!

"You know, you should go out and buy a lottery ticket", the doctor remarked. I asked why. She explained that I was fortunate to be in a hospital environment when delivering my baby. She explained that with 'placenta percreta', I had the highest mortality rate for a mother in childbirth. If I had been at home going through natural labor, my daughter would have had only six minutes to be born without oxygen deprivation. And not only that, I myself would have probably bled out in 20 minutes.

She continued. "Do you remember when you were in the ER a few weeks back? It was me that was planning to come the next morning to do 'exploratory surgery'. I suspected you might have had a hernia. But you left for some reason and signed a waiver."

Then it hit me. Divine intervention had to have happened. This time the hair stood up on my arms! Chills ran up my spine! If it hadn't been for the *'rudeness of a stranger'* and that nurse hadn't said what she said, my daughter probably would have not survived the surgery that day!

This truly was a miracle in the synchronicity of events that occurred. This wasn't an accident. This was the real deal – a genuine, authentic unexpected *'miracle'*. And where do miracles come from? To me, there is no question. I believe devoutly in God and I *know* that he had a hand in *'nudging'* that nurse to say what she did. Call it what you will, but this to me is empirical proof of *'Divine Intervention'!*

CHAPTER SEVEN – RECOVERY & REFLECTION

Have you ever wondered about how things seem to happen for a reason? They say that synchronicity is a connection that happens in a timely way. Synchronicity also usually clusters around significant events. These meaningful connections, when they occur, guide us, warn us or confirm us on our path. Coincidence occurs or happens at a specific moment.

There's no question that synchronicity and coincidences are regarded as everyday events that occur. Usually, we take them for granted. Not much serious thought is given to them at the time they take place. It's only afterward when one has the time to reflect, that a bigger picture emerges.

The Butterfly Effect

In 2004, a science fiction thriller was written and directed by Eric Bress and J. Mackye Gruber. It starred Ashton Kutcher and Amy Smart. *The Butterfly Effect*, for those who are not familiar with the term, involves how everything is interconnected. It is a popular, hypothetical theory which illustrates how small initial differences may lead to large unforeseen consequences over the course of time. It is a metaphor for how a small and insignificant event in the past can cause a major change in circumstances in the future. The plot of this movie was the ability to go back in time and change one minor incident to change the trajectory of the future outcome.

I didn't experience *'The Butterfly Effect'*. I experienced the profound impact of how *'God's hand'* caused and orchestrated a series of calculated events that could be described only as divine *'blessings in disguise.'* And more importantly, I began to truly understand the magnitude of every event that takes place on our own personal timeline.

The Butterfly Effect vs God's Hands

CHAPTER EIGHT – DISCOVERED BLESSINGS IN DISGUISE

On February 3, 1998, I was released from the hospital after two long weeks and was able to return home. At first, I just allowed myself to simply bask in the comfort of being at home. I knew how lucky we were to be alive, and I never once questioned the hand of *'God'* playing a major role in the miraculous outcome that took place.

But with time at home, I was now able to fully reflect and consider all that had happened in the previous 16 months. During that next six months in post-partum recovery, I went on an intentional inward self-journey. I wanted to embrace all that had taken place and wanted to understand. In so doing, I discovered startling revelations that can only be described as a series of *'blessings in disguise'*.

Be patient with me while I attempt to explain my humble insights. I promise you, it shall be very eye-opening and enlightening.

1. I was born on February 4, 1957. I am the third of nine children. All my brothers and sisters were born in natural delivery including me. But I was a difficult delivery for my poor Mother. You see I was 'breech' or 'turned the other way'.

Is it a coincidence that I too bore not one, but all three daughters breech?!?... I wonder.

2. At age 30, I married my husband. We met at work. Abed wanted to take me out from day one. But... I had this policy

not to date anyone I worked with. That said, two years later, he unexpectedly stopped the elevator after our dinner break (we worked the night shift) and told me, "Okay, you have no other choice but to go out with me now." He had just landed a big promotion which forced him to be transferred to the day shift.

Each of us has our own TIMELINE...

- Image by Dim Loic© on Unsplash©

Long story short, we ended up getting engaged six months later. Four months after that, we were happily married. Why is this significant? You will see momentarily.

3. On July 8, 1990, I became a proud mother delivering my first daughter, Renae Patricia. I was all set and prepared to go through natural labor (with the aid of an epidural of course!) This did not turn out to be the case. Patty, as she was dearly called, was a breech presentation. Because we had great insurance coverage, a C-section was performed.

4. It took over 5 ½ years and several bouts of various infertility drugs to become pregnant with my next child. I would be 40 when giving birth. Becoming pregnant alone was a miracle itself.

5. This time, due to insurance limitations, I was advised that I would be delivering wonderful Layla Saphia naturally. This is known as a V-BAC, otherwise known as vaginal birth after a C-section. Layla was also a breech presentation on the normal sonogram. But instead of immediately agreeing to a C-section, the insurance company wanted to attempt a 'turning' to prevent having to do the more expensive surgery. It was not to be. After one hour of torturous manipulation, I said 'enough is enough'. Two hours later, Layla was born via C-Section. Another miraculous day occurring on May 6, 1996.

6. While hospice-caring for my dying mother, my husband made a surprise trip to Missouri bringing my first daughter Patty. I did the math later, finding out the incredible news of being pregnant again! It became quite obvious when wonderful Nadean was conceived.

7. I have to confess I wasn't very keen concerning my doctor who cared for me during the entire time I was pregnant. I recall, on more than one occasion, of complaining of abdominal pain during my routine checkups. I was totally dismissed each time, by either himself or one of the attending nurses. They would explain it away by saying it was because I was just an old mother. And as such, it was to be expected to have all sorts of various aches and pains. They were nothing to worry about they insisted each time I brought it up.

Little did I know at the time, it was a good thing they dismissed me. I did what they told me, and I just always returned home and took it easy... And you know what? I'm so glad I did.

8. If you recall in chapter one, I discussed what my last sonogram was like. I shall remind you. The sonographer took over 20 minutes and when I asked why it was taking so long and if anything was wrong. She quickly said, "No, everything is fine. Your baby is fully developed and healthy." "I'm just trying to find the origination of the placenta." She knew. Oh yes, she and my doctor knew…

9. As a result of having two previous C-sections and of the placenta percreta (unbeknown to me at the time), I was immediately scheduled for my third C-section. This surgery took place three full weeks before I reached full term. That is why I found myself in a hospital environment on Tuesday, January 20, 1998. Had I NOT been in a hospital environment with an immediate surgical team on hand, I would not be sitting here in Star Bucks typing this manuscript.

10. Do you remember earlier when I told you that the Anesthesiologist insisted that I have a spinal block instead of the epidural? Well… come to find out after-the-fact, there was a definite reason for that!

   Now I'm not a medical expert by any means. But the reason the spinal block was the preferred method of anesthesiology, had to do with how it was both administered and the effects of it. I was told later while in the ICU by that same Anesthesiologist that it was the better decision to have been on the spinal block and NOT the epidural as further complications could have occurred.

11. Even being afflicted with post-partum depression played a major role in these profound discoveries. Why? Because

the recovery process took time and frequently feeling alone and isolated, I spent most of that time at home. You may be perplexed as to why I have this listed as well. Trust me, you will soon see why.

12. The list goes on and on… When I look over these past incidents I described above, I feel so grateful for each and every one of them. In fact, I'm eternally grateful for everything in my life today.

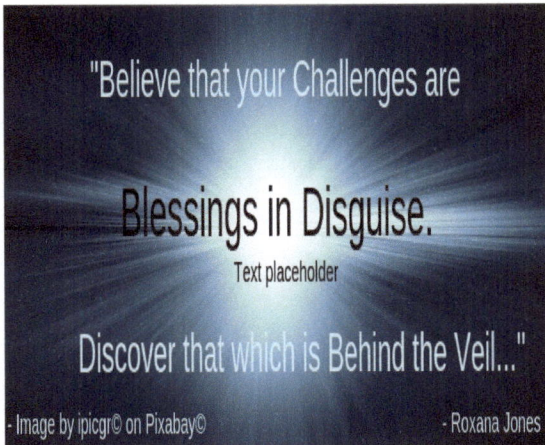

"Believe that your Challenges are

Blessings in Disguise.

Text placeholder

Discover that which is Behind the Veil..."

- Image by ipicgr© on Pixabay©   - Roxana Jones

CHAPTER NINE – LIFE-CHANGING REALIZATIONS

I came away with two very powerful realizations. One, the indisputable and empirical fact that *God is real.* Very real. It was actually just another confirmation of this since I already had this enlightenment when my Mother had passed the year before. But this time around, it was more than that. It was this feeling of *'knowing'* that *God* is ever-present and everywhere at any given moment in our lives.

Two, there is no denying that the miraculous birth of my daughter, Nadean and I myself, were brought into this world for a reason. And none of this would have taken place if even one single event had not occurred. And for the most part, one would have to agree that individually considered, these events could be looked at as just 'normal everyday' happenings.

We are ALL Miracles

We are all a miracle. Each of us is uniquely special and even the date of our birth is of significant importance. When my next birthday came around, an overwhelming sense of urgency came over me to find out the odds of being born. I took to the internet and (coincidentally or not…) I came across this quote:

"A miracle is an event so unlikely as to be almost impossible. By that definition, I've just proven that you are a miracle."
By Dr. Ali Binazir

Dear readers. Do me a favor and go back a second time and re-read that powerful statement and quote.

Did it send chills down your spine? Because it should. Going further, I happened to come across a YouTube video featuring Mel Gibbons. She is a well-known author and motivational speaker. I was perusing the Ted Talks series at the time. This organization is known for their influential talks and videos. Their mission statement is to inform the public of "ideas worth sharing". This is what Mel Gibbons conveyed:

"You are One in 400 Trillion"

Think about it. The probability of you even being born on this planet is one in 400 trillion. More precisely, this is the probability of you just being born. But the odds of being born with your particular parents AND with your particular genetic make-up or DNA is a whole other chapter. I could easily finish my book here and simply reiterate that unexpected miracles happen every day. I could also just reiterate that each of us is a miracle all in itself.

But I'm not done yet. This is far too important to end my story here. It is vital that each and every one who reads this book truly understand who you are. You see as Mel Gibbons stated, it's not just about the odds of being born, it's something much more. More than we can hardly comprehend.

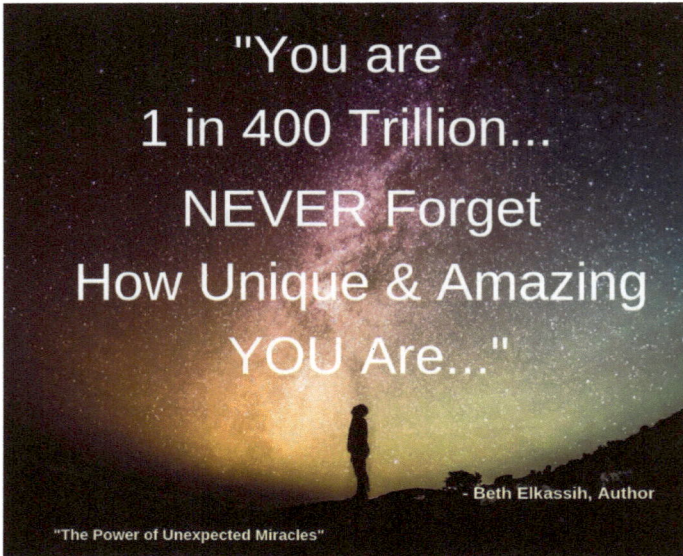

"You are
1 in 400 Trillion...
NEVER Forget
How Unique & Amazing
YOU Are..."

- Beth Elkassih, Author

"The Power of Unexpected Miracles"

Even the 'Birthdate' is of Major Importance!

It's about who your parents are. It's about where you were born. It's about the date and even the time. It's about who you marry. It's about who your grandparents are, who your great-grandparents are, who your aunts and uncles are and yes, even who your cousins and friends are.

How did I figure this out? Let me share with you how I know.

Remember when I was going through all the series of events that occurred in my timeline? These are without question, examples of *'blessings in disguise'.* But when I dug even further, I discovered even more preponderance of evidence proving Divine Intervention definitely exists.

The first 'blessing in disguise' I wrote about was simply my birthdate being February 4, 1957. I wasn't born in 1400 or 1800 or even 1956 for that matter. No, this date wasn't an accident. It was intentional and divinely orchestrated to be that precise moment in time.

If I hadn't been predisposed on my mother's side to have 'breech babies', then none of this would have taken place.

If I hadn't been in my 40s at the time; if it hadn't been 1998 when I gave birth and instead it was even 1960, I would have found myself more than likely at home going through intensive labor. If it hadn't been for the fact that the birth of my child was in modern day 20st century; if it hadn't been for current state-of-the-art technology evolution at that time; if it hadn't been for the fact of living near an urban community with significantly improved medical facilities, Nadean Elizabeth would NOT BE HERE.

And yes, my friends, if it hadn't been for the fact that I experienced and suffered through post-partum depression, giving me the much needed time to reflect and determine this incredible life-changing epiphany, I probably wouldn't have come to this divine enlightenment. Yes, I needed to include this as another 'blessings in disguise'.

So, have I made it clear yet! My dear readers, we are truly 'divine miracle beings'. And I believe we are here for a purpose. I believe it is to be the best we can be. I believe we are to be kind and nonjudgmental to all. I believe we are to be forgiving and to love one another. I believe we are to be role models and spread the good word to everyone we meet. I believe this is our calling to strengthen our own faith in GOD.

I believe as I'm sitting here typing this manuscript, this is also what I have been led to do. I believe in the power of unexpected miracles. And it is my desire, if not my duty, to convey this power-ful message to as many souls as I can.

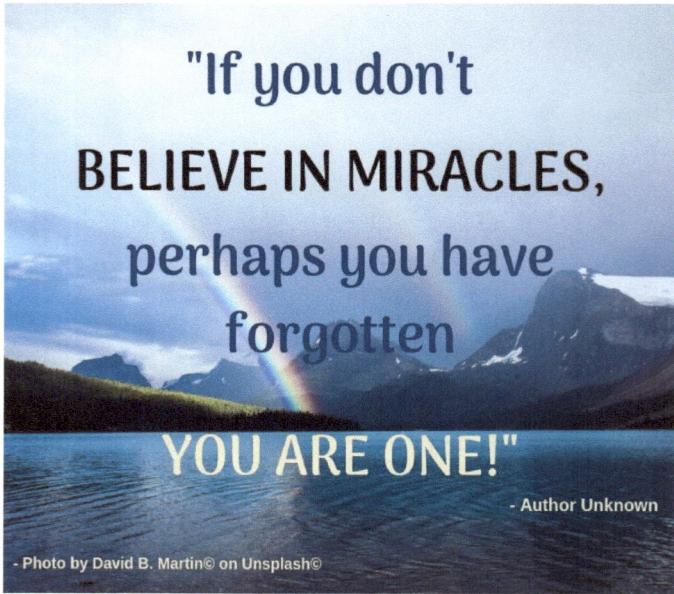

"If you don't
BELIEVE IN MIRACLES,
perhaps you have
forgotten
YOU ARE ONE!"
- Author Unknown

- Photo by David B. Martin© on Unsplash©

CHAPTER TEN – IN CONCLUSION

Hopefully, you can now embrace *'The Power of Unexpected Miracles'* and celebrate it in your own life. I invite you to really go inside yourself and reflect on your own personal life and timeline.

Perhaps there's been more than one occasion when you've wondered why things happened the way they did. I encourage you to ponder times in the past when you felt you were treated badly or given the short end of the stick. What about the good times? What about your marriage, the birth of your children, or even meeting someone new in the grocery store? What possible *'unexpected miracles'* could have happened along the way to arrive at those joyous occasions?

So… the next time you overhear someone making a rude comment, please remember reading this book. Try not to be so judgmental. Let us all be forgiving and take a step back. There just might be a *'divine miracle'* in the works!

The End

"Once you believe in yourself and see your soul as divine and precious, you'll automatically be converted to a being who believes in Miracles!"

- Wayne W. Dyer

- Photo by Abigail Keenan© on Unsplash©

ABOUT THE AUTHOR

Beth Elkassih is a professional blogger and creator of the inspirational website, "Made You Smile Back". Her heartfelt passion is to inspire and motivate people to become their personal best. She is also actively involved in mental health advocacy and is a Realtor in the Dallas/Fort Worth TX metroplex.

She is married and has 3 daughters. She is one of nine children and was raised in the Midwest from rural Shelby County, Missouri. She is also available for motivational speaking and can be contacted via her email at beth@madeyousmileback.com

THANK YOU FOR READING MY BOOK!

Thank you for allowing me to share my personal journey with you on the miraculous series of events that led up to my daughter's birth. If you enjoyed *"The Power of Unexpected Miracles",* please consider telling your friends or posting a short review. It would mean a lot to me. I also welcome you to visit my website: https://madeyousmileback.com where you can enjoy both inspirational and thought-provoking content on a daily basis.

Plans are in the works for additional books including a companion book entitled, 'Miracle Power Quotes'' as well as "Unexpected Miracles Happen Everyday" which shall be a collection of individual stories of miracles from ordinary people who have extraordinary events. A collaboration for an exciting and much needed book dealing with post-partum depression is also forthcoming. Be sure to subscribe to my blog so you can be the first to know about upcoming pre-release dates.

Share on Social Media

Please visit 'Made You Smile Back' via their social media websites:

f /madeyousmileback   **P** /madeyousmileback
🐦 /madesmileback   **📷** /madeyousmileback

On the behalf of Believe In Your Dreams Publishing, we would like to express an abundance of gratitude, love, and blessings to Beth Elkassih. Thank you for trusting Believe In Your Dreams Publishing and Production team with your amazing project. May your book bring out MIRACLES all across the globe.

Believe In Your Dreams Publishing would like to extend further appreciation to every reader who purchase a copy of this amazing book. I pray each story will touch and heal the lives of many people across this great nation. Thanks for believing in me and my rocking team. We love, adore, and appreciate you all.

~ CEO, Nichole Peters

Believe In Your Dreams Publishing